Church of England, Archdeaconry of Dorset, Thomas
Sanctuary

A Charge of the Archdeacon of Dorset

delivered to the clergy and churchwardens at his visitation in June, 1874 -

to which is appended a plea for toleration by law in certain ritual matters

Church of England, Archdeaconry of Dorset, Thomas Sanctuary

A Charge of the Archdeacon of Dorset
*delivered to the clergy and churchwardens at his visitation in June, 1874 - to which
is appended a plea for toleration by law in certain ritual matters*

ISBN/EAN: 9783337284985

Printed in Europe, USA, Canada, Australia, Japan

Cover: Foto ©Lupo / pixelio.de

More available books at **www.hansebooks.com**

A CHARGE

OF

ℭhe Archdeacon of Dorset,

DELIVERED TO THE

CLERGY

AND

CHURCHWARDENS

AT HIS VISITATION

IN

JUNE, 1874;

TO WHICH IS APPENDED

A Plea for Toleration by Law in certain Ritual Matters with Reference to "The Public Worship Regulation Bill."

By THE BISHOP OF LINCOLN.

Dorchester :
H. SPICER, COUNTY PRINTER.
1874

A copy of this Charge is with great respect presented to each of the Clergy and of the Church-wardens of the Archdeaconry of Dorset by their faithful friend and brother the Archdeacon, with his special request that they will give very careful consideration to the weighty words of the Bishop of Lincoln, which are given in the Appendix, and on which the Archdeacon's own remarks upon the Ritual matters in question are for the most part founded.

Powerstock,
    July 3rd, 1874.

THE ARCHDEACON'S CHARGE.

My Reverend Brethren and my Brethren of the Laity,
—I propose to speak to you chiefly with reference to
subjects which have lately come before us in our
Diocesan Synod or in Convocation. The fact that these
matters have been under consideration in those assemblies is an evidence that they are of present interest,
and it arises out of our due relation to those higher
Synods of the Church that in these subordinate assemblies we should record the decisions which have there
been given, and treat of those things which have there
been set forth for the consideration of the Church. In
this way we may, on the one hand, in our own localities,
make known and promote the adoption of measures
which have been, as it were, sent down to us ; and, on
the other, we may have our part in securing a just
settlement of things that are not yet determined. I
will therefore make a few remarks upon some of these
subjects, in the hope of leading you to give them further
consideration individually, and in ruri-decanal chapters
and meetings—and this with a view to having the conclusions so arrived at sent up either in petitions presented
or words spoken by those who represent you in the
Diocesan Synod or in Convocation. For neither the one
assembly nor the other is competent to give a sound and
final decision upon questions on which the mind of the
faithful members of the Church has not been, more or
less, previously ascertained and declared.

And, first, I would say a few words in reference to the

PUBLIC WORSHIP REGULATION BILL.

The subject with which it deals has been placed before
the Convocations both of Canterbury and York, but, in
my judgment, in the wrong form, at the wrong time,
and with too little opportunity for it to receive mature
consideration. The mind of the Church had not been
ascertained when the Bill was introduced. Churchmen

generally were taken by surprise. The powers of the State were invoked for a settlement of religious questions which had not first been weighed and determined upon by the Spiritualty of the realm. All must, I think, be agreed that the constitution and modes of procedure of our Ecclesiastical Courts require amendment ; for, only to take one point, it is intolerable that the redress of a grievance should only be attainable, as is now continually the case, at the cost of thousands of pounds ; and no one can deny that a remedy is urgently needed for evils and abuses prevailing in some of our churches in the ritual of Divine service, whether by excess or defect. But I think it is right for those who hold the opinion to express it—and it has been very widely expressed—that before a new enactment is made by the State to enforce the law of the Church we ought to have some determination by the Church of what, upon some important matters, that law is which is to be enforced. I think it is not untruly said that "it is beginning at the wrong end to simplify ecclesiastical proceedings till the *mos* or *lex* which has to be administered is rather more clearly defined. The process of court-making might otherwise be represented as one for forcing rather than working out a ceremonial system." The pleadings of that learned, holy, and truly Anglo-Catholic Bishop of Lincoln have carried conviction to my own mind of the soundness of his "Plea for Toleration by Law in certain Ritual Matters with reference to the Public Worship Regulation Bill." The proposition which the Bishop has there made is of serious importance, and probably he is the one man more than any other competent to make it. This, however, is certain—that concerning some pressing questions of Ritual it has to be determined, as a matter of first concern and requiring a settlement not long deferred, whether with just regard to truth the claim of charity can be allowed. The eastward position of the celebrant at the prayer of consecration in the Holy Communion is perhaps the principal point in question. It is for a concession of liberty in respect of this position that a very earnest appeal is made by many zealous and loyal clergy and by many who do not take that position themselves. It is my own conviction that the rubric, rightly interpreted, orders the clergy to " break the bread before the people" —in such a way "before the people" that the appointed sign of breaking the bread may be so made as to be within sight of the people—and consequently that the eastward position of the celebrant is not the position which the Church of England intended her clergy to

take. And this, in the opinion of the Bishop of Lincoln, may probably be the decision of the final court; and perhaps it may not be out of place to mention that Bishop Hamilton took this interpretation of the rubric as the guide for his own practice. Moreover, a very large number of the clergy—and I am myself one of the number—believe that not only in respect of the rubric, but upon ground apart from the letter of the Prayer Book, the eastward position is not the better way, and it is a position which they would not themselves willingly adopt. But with all this it must still be borne in mind that, not to mention arguments of more or less weight which are adduced in favour of the eastward position, it is evident that the matter is not explicit and simple in law. Some very remarkable words in respect of the legal position of the question have been very lately spoken by a man who will not be accused of disloyalty to the Reformation, and whose authority as a lawyer is beyond question—the present Lord Chancellor, Lord Cairns. And his words concur with those of another man of like high legal authority. He says :—
"As to the position of the minister in the Communion service during the time of consecration, that is a subject on which it will not be expected, nor would it be proper, that I should give any expression of opinion as to what the law on the subject may be. But I wish to call your lordships' attention to the position of the question. I think that there are in the Church of England a great number of persons—a large number of clergymen— who have no sympathy whatever with Ritualists—I use a familiar expression—or Ritualism, who have no sympathy with those extravagances and those departures from the law that have been referred to in this House, and who yet feel themselves much distressed and dis-quieted by the present law on the subject of the position of the minister during the time of consecration. Upon that subject there have been two decisions, more or less final, by the Judicial Committee of the Privy Council. I do not desire to say one word as to the law on the question, but every one knows how extremely difficult it is for any person—for any layman, perhaps for any lawyer—to be satisfied that those two decisions are reconcileable with each other. In one of those cases no defence was made, and only one side was heard. *Those decisions, I think, cannot be regarded as final"*— very weighty words. And he goes on to give a sign of approval to the suggestion of the Bishop of Peterborough, a suggestion founded upon the plea for toleration of the Bishop of Lincoln—that this question should be placed

upon neutral ground. But we must take note of the
vital distinction there is between the proposal of the
Bishop of Peterborough which was adopted by the Lord
Chancellor and now happily withdrawn, and that of the
Bishop of Lincoln. In the former case, to use the Lord
Chancellor's description of the plan, he is reported to say
"I see in the proposal of the Right Reverend Prelate
much that in a rough way would arrive at a conclusion
which for practical purposes is not unlike conclusions
which might be arrived at by rubrical alterations."
Now this rough way of arriving at conclusions for
practical purposes in Parliament upon serious questions
of religion may commend itself to some minds, but it is
not the thing recommended by the Bishop of Lincoln.
In his plea for toleration—after deprecating its being
left to individual clergymen to choose by an eclectic
process what rites and ceremonies they please from
ancient, mediæval, or modern Churches, and to import them into their own Churches and to impose
them on their own congregations—the Bishop says
"The Church of England, exercising that authority
which belongs to all National Churches, ought to define
and declare publicly by her synodical judgments what
things in her services are to be regarded as obligatory
and what may be considered as indifferent. And she
ought, as an Established Church, to seek for legal
sanction from the Crown and from Parliament for these
her authoritative definitions and declarations. These
were the principles on which our Book of Common
Prayer was framed and revised." And in his place
in the House of Lords, among much else to the same
effect, the Bishop is reported to have said "In order that
legislation might be effective, that it might produce
harmony and not discord, it was absolutely necessary
that it should carry with it the sympathy of the clergy
of the Church of England. The clergy of the Church
of England exercised an influence—not only spiritual
and religious, but moral and political—over the great
body of the English community. It would be an evil
day for the Legislature and for the Government, but
still more for the Church itself, if the clergy were to be
alienated in feeling from the civil authorities in the
State. Leaving out of view the men of extreme opinions,
he was in a position to state that the clergy were
alarmed, not by this Bill alone, but also by the manner
in which it was carried forward. It seemed to him that
the obvious means of conciliating the clergy was to
consult the Synods in which they were represented."
And he added " If that body were consulted in a proper

way I am persuaded that hardly a week would elapse before a peaceful solution of the difficulty had been arrived at." This course of procedure, whatever persons of high authority in the State may say to the contrary, I conceive to be the only legitimate one—the only one to which any religious body can, with justice to itself, submit. If toleration by law can be had in this orderly way it is, in my judgment, a thing to be much desired, and it is a course, as we have been reminded, which has been taken by the Protestant Episcopal Church of America, a Church in full communion with ourselves. The question cannot much longer be left in uncertainty and it remains for those who preside over the Church of England to call upon her to determine whether she can rightly pronounce that the position of the celebrant at the Prayer of Consecration in the Holy Communion is a thing in itself indifferent or not. This I feel—that some part of the special significance of the one position and the other would be removed if by the authority of the law both positions were made equally lawful. I must here mention that I have in my possession a letter of that great Bishop, whose loss the whole Church of England so deeply feels—Bishop Wilberforce—which touches very closely upon this point. I had written to him about a friend of mine who had applied to him for the appointment to an important curacy, and had said in the letter, in which I strongly commended this clergyman to the Bishop in all other respects, that I was not certain whether he might not make it a point of conscience to take the eastward position at the Holy Communion, and that I felt it right to mention this. And the reply that came from the Bishop to my friend contained these words—"The only point in the Archdeacon's letter which suggests any difficulty is what appears to me *a very immaterial question*—namely, as to where you stand at the Prayer of Consecration. As to that, it is absolutely necessary that the curate conforms to the custom of the Church. Which way that is I am not absolutely certain." I have said enough to express my own desire that the Church should in her convocations and in her other assemblies anxiously consider whether this liberty can rightly be conceded. And the solution which I should myself hope to see is that which the Bishop of Lincoln proposes—" Let either position of the celebrant be declared by authority to be lawful ; in other words, let the position be pronounced by law to be indifferent." And again with him as to that other matter which is in dispute at law, I feel constrained to say—"Let the

National Church of England declare by authority that a simple distinctive dress for the celebration of the Holy Eucharist is permissible, but not to be enforced upon any. This also has already been done in some dioceses of America. In that country there is a double safeguard against extravagances; first, the consent, duly ascertained and expressed, of the communicants of the congregation or parish; and next, the sanction of the Ordinary. Both these guarantees against innovations and excesses may be obtained in the Church of England as well as in that of America." With respect to the position of this question at law, the Bishop says, "I am rather disposed to think that the use of such a vestment might hereafter be pronounced to be obligatory." I think Mr. Beresford Hope states the position of this question fairly. He says "As to the distinctive dress at the Holy Communion, the question has really been brought within a very narrow compass. A prescription of such dresses applying to all churches is unquestionably found in a rubric of the Prayer Book of 1549, and is, as many contend, re-enacted in the existing Ornaments Rubric. Another prescription of such dresses—(which may either be (1) supplementary to that rubric, and intended to enforce a minimum of compliance with it, or else (2) falling short of it, and intended to supplant it), only mentioning their use in cathedrals and collegiate churches—is found in the 24th and 25th Canons of 1603. The judicial committee, in *Hibbert* v. *Purchas*, rejected the wider prescription of the dresses contained in the rubric, but re-affirmed the narrower one of the canons; and since that judgment several distinguished prelates and dignitaries have adopted such dresses under the conditions which the canons lay down. But the principle underlying the rubric of 1549 and the canons of 1603 is confessedly the same—that of doing the highest material honour to Almighty God at the highest act of worship. Thus the question is reduced to a very narrow issue, not of principle, but of detail. "Does the 24th Canon contemplate a maximum or a minimum use of the given ceremonial? At this point, surely, negotiation may come in." And what is the principle which underlies the whole ordering of our Prayer Book? It is affirmed in the preface, where it is said "It has been the wisdom of the Church of England, ever since the first compiling of her public liturgy, to keep the mean between the two extremes, of too much stiffness in refusing, and of too much laxness in admitting, any variation from it;" and "it is but reasonable that, upon weighty and important considerations, according to the various exigencies of times and occasions, such changes and alterations should be made therein as to those that are in places of authority should from time to time seem either necessary or expedient." And upon this the Bishop of Lincoln remarks :—"It may, therefore, be presumed that our reformers and our revisers of the Book of Common Prayer would, as wise, learned, and pious men, carefully contemplating the altered circumstances of the time and the condition of the Church in these days, be the first to relax some of the stringent laws of our ritual, and to pronounce certain things to be indifferent by law, in order that they might promote those high and holy purposes of faith, worship, and morals for which the Prayer Book was framed, and which are paramount to all rites and ceremonies of human institutions." With regard to the Bill itself, it is so altered that its original features can scarcely be recognised, and as I write this it is hard to ascertain what its present form is—much less to give an opinion as to what it may become before it passes, if indeed it does this year pass into law. Whatever may be its final shape it may, in my opinion, be taken for certain that, after all that has taken place, no proceedings under it will be allowed either in respect of things doubtful in law or of things which may before long be pronounced indifferent. The bishops, it seems, are to have a discretion in allowing proceedings to be taken ; and it is very unlikely they will encourage litigation. I trust that they will not consent to part with anything which of right belongs to them as rulers in their own dioceses, subject to the higher provincial rule of the Archbishop, and, as a last resort, to the Final Court of Appeal. An ecclesiastical lawyer—a man at the summit of his profession—said to me a few days since " You do not want new courts ; you want to simplify, cheapen, and expedite the course of procedure in the courts which you already have." But I will not weary you with more about this great legal problem. Believing as I do that the mind of the great body of the Church of England is sound and right, I believe also that by the care of Him who is ever with us we shall be safely guided through our present difficulties.

THE PAN-ANGLICAN SYNOD.

I should like just to say that in my opinion some of the most grave questions which are now before the Church will rightly be brought under consideration when there is another conference of the Bishops of the Anglican Communion, and that such a conference, which will probably soon be held, will be likely to conduce beyond anything else to a settlement of things in which all the Churches of one communion are equally interested with ourselves. The Bishop of Lichfield lately presented a memorial from the Bishops of the Ecclesiastical Province of Canada and from the West Indian Bishops to the Archbishop of Canterbury (and this memorial is supported by the wishes of the United States' and Australian Churches), praying for this conference; and the Archbishop has appointed a joint committee of both Houses of Convocation to report to him upon (1) his own relation to the various branches of the Anglican communion scattered throughout the world and upon (2) the petition of the bishops. And among other words upon this subject, speaking with that breadth of view and largeness of heart which so characterise him, Bishop Selwyn said:—"Even though there is no probability of the unity of Christendom being restored, is it for us to sit down in despair, or, rather, ought we not to thank God that He has already spread the Anglican communion throughout so large a portion of the earth, and that there is power now by united action and the blessing of the Holy Spirit of seeking for that spiritual control which, in the early ages, pronounced authoritatively on all disputed questions? Having nearly 160 Bishops who preside over the Anglican Communion, I am persuaded that a voluntary tribunal of appeal, established by their authority under the presidency of the Archbishop of Canterbury, would be accepted as a court of final appeal on questions of doctrine now threatening the disruption of various branches of the Church. It would be the central magnet by which all the planetary bodies that revolve round the Church of England would be kept in subjection. I should like to speak as to the probable effect of the existence of such a body. I cannot hope that any very great result will come from the rigid enforcement of laws laid down in language, often ambiguous, 200 or 300 years ago. I cannot believe that it was ever intended that the laws then made should never admit of any contemporaneous exposition by the voice of the Church, but should be submitted to the law courts to be judged by the verbal and literal construction of legal documents. What I do gather from the opinions of many of the most intelligent of the clergy is that if the authoritative voice of the Church itself could be heard there is scarcely one clergyman in a thousand who would not respect it. There are some who deny the authority of the Judicial Committee of the Privy Council, and some who doubt

whether its doctrines are good ; and whilst that state of
doubt remains clergymen are tempted to wander into
the dark regions of so-called Catholicity to seek for
reasons to justify disobedience to the law ; and raise,
upon grounds wholly insufficient, the question whether
they ought not to obey God rather than man. I lament
the existence of this state of mind, but when doubts of
that kind exist it is our duty to seek the remedy ; and
instead of attempting to enforce the law I think much
more would be done by establishing such a tribunal as
that which I have pointed out, which should take into
consideration statements of doctrine, and external acts
symbolical of doctrine, and decide whether such words
and acts are or are not permissible to a priest of the
Church of England in any branch of the Anglican
Communion. If such a tribunal were established I
could mention some who would give their willing sub-
mission to the authoritative voice of the Church
declared in the manner which I have endeavoured to
describe, especially if that voice came from the united
Anglican Communion, under the presidency of the
Archbishop of Canterbury."

NEW CODE OF CANONS.

It comes in here to mention that a committee of Convocation was appointed by the President in 1866 "to
examine the constitutions and canons ecclesiastical with a
view to their amendment and adaptation to the present
necessities of the Church." Afterwards enlarged powers
were given to the committee, and it was instructed to
prepare and submit to the House a body of new canons,
and they have co-operated in their deliberations and in
their work with a Committee of the Convocation of
York. We need not dwell on the necessity of a code of
canons suitable to these times, for such necessity is
manifest to any one who reads carefully the canons to
which we owe allegiance now. The joint committee
has just lately brought to a final completion a work
which, as they say, has cost many of them days and
even years of anxiety and labour. They have issued a
draft of a new code of canons, and in presenting it to
the House they say—"It will be for the Convocations
of the two Provinces to enlarge and amend in substance
and in form the canons suggested in this attempt ;
but the committee are not without hope that, if the
House will apply to the Crown for license to enact a
new body of canons, the draft which follows this report
may at least form a guide to the deliberations of this
House, and perhaps a foundation on which to build a

useful structure of Church practice. The committee
would only further suggest that the accompanying
draft of a new code of canons should be printed, and, if
possible, obtain some extended circulation among the
clergy and others of both Provinces, in order that the
opinion and judgment of the Church at large should be
in some degree obtained before a discussion of the
separate canons takes place in the House of Convocation.
The committee, in conclusion, desire to lay this their
report before the House, with an earnest prayer that
the anxious and laborious work of several years may be
some help to this Synod in promoting the order and
efficiency of Christ's Kingdom in England." The Dean
of Winchester is the chairman of this committee, and in
a letter which I lately received from him he says—"Our
present object is to get this draft so far into circulation that
we may obtain the general opinion of Churchmen before the
subject is taken up in Convocation, and it would do the
committee real service if by any means you can make
this known." It will be seen that the matter is of great
importance, and that it is one which could, to great
advantage, be brought before our ruri-decanal chapters—
and it would, I think, be a good thing to have a number
of copies of this draft printed in a cheap form for
circulation among the clergy and others in the archdeaconry, in order to make known what is proposed,
and to elicit the mind of the Church upon the
proposals. The last canon in the draft entitled "Of
obedience to Canons Ecclesiastical" sets forth the
relation in which Churchmen stand to them.
"Canons, constitutions, and ordinances, being rules set
forth in this Church by those who have authority thereto,
for the direction and good government of the Church,
and for the framing of the lives and conduct both of
the clergy and of the lay members thereof in accordance
with right discipline and the law of Christ, are not only
to be yielded unto at such times as they are put in force
by the spiritual courts, but also ought to be obeyed and
kept dutifully and conscientiously by every member of
this Church, following with a free will and glad mind
the godly rules and order out of the same." It will be
seen that this settlement of a new code of canons,
thus claiming our obedience, must be considered in
connection with the review of the rubrics and of the law
which is to regulate our public worship.

ECCLESIASTICAL DILAPIDATIONS.

To the subject of Ecclesiastical Dilapidations—a
subject very different indeed in kind from those of

which we have been speaking—I have, in my circular letter, called your special attention, because it is one in which very many of us have a direct practical interest, because I have had some letters from the clergy on the subject, and also because the Acts by which arrangements are now made in this matter are not held to contain a final settlement of the question. There is a report of a Committee of Convocation on the subject which has not yet been taken into consideration, and there have been several petitions to Convocation containing *gravamina* in the matter, and these have been referred to the committee which at the commencement of this present Convocation was re-appointed by the Archbishop. The committee have "to consider and report whether any, and if any, what alterations might advantageously be made in the laws relating to dilapidations of ecclesiastical buildings." I will shortly place before you some of the points upon which suggestions for alteration have been made, not by any means thinking them all equally good, but with the thought that it might be well perhaps if in our ruri-decanal chapters we, were to consider these and any other particulars of the question. We must be all agreed that the old system was not good for the property of the Church, and not good for the clergy and their families. The intention of the Act of 1871 was better to ensure ecclesiastical buildings from decay, to improve the method of the assessment of dilapidations, and in other ways to give relief. And no doubt much good in respect of the first object has been effected. Already the property of the Church has been greatly benefited by the requirement that in every case of sequestration, and in every case of a benefice becoming vacant, either by resignation, exchange, or death, the buildings must, as soon as circumstances admit, be put into thorough repair. In the case of a vacant benefice the claim for dilapidations stands on the same footing as other debts, but if the estate of the late incumbent is insufficient to meet the claim, facilities are given to the new incumbent, who is called upon to repair the dilapidations, to borrow money from Queen Anne's Bounty. Many too of the uncertainties and abuses of the old system have been removed. These we will not discuss, but turn to some things which have been suggested as amendments of the present law. And (1) the Committee of Convocation recommend that power should be given to the Governors of Queen Anne's Bounty to frame rules and regulations for the guidance of surveyors and other persons who have to carry the provisions of the Act into operation. This is one thing for which I think we ought to press. At present there is much left to the judgment of the several surveyors. There have, for instance, been conflicting opinions upon the most important question of what they term 'insensible waste'—that is, gradual deterioration of property by fair wear and tear—as to what it is and how it should be dealt with. Is it not desirable that the law should lay down some definite principles in this particular for the guidance of the surveyors and for the Bishop who by the Act has to give the final decision when the surveyor's report is disputed? Then (2) there is the question of insurance. By the Act every incumbent is to insure against fire in the joint names of himself and the governors (to at least three-fifths of their value) all the buildings which he is liable to repair, and he is to exhibit the receipt for the premium of such insurance every year at the visitation of the Bishop or Archdeacon, and the following questions are to be added to those annually sent to incumbents under the provisions of the Act of the Session of the first and second years of Her Majesty, chapter one hundred and six, that is to say :—" In what office, and for what amount, are the buildings of your benefice insured against fire? And what was the amount and date of the last annual payment for such insurance?" Apart from the claim for obedience to its provisions made by the Act there is the penalty that in case of loss by fire, and an insufficiency of insurance to meet the loss, the surveyor has to give the Bishop a certificate stating the extent of the deficiency, and the incumbent has within three months to pay the deficiency, on the pain of having his living sequestered. We shall, I think, be agreed that the holders of Church property in trust should be under an obligation to ensure that property against fire, and it is suggested by the Convocation Committee that the governors of Queen Anne's Bounty be empowered to effect these insurances, and that all new incumbents be obliged to ensure with the said governors. They put this suggestion in the following form :—" The premiums might be paid by the clergy as the tenths now are, and be recoverable by the governors in the same way. The facilities which the office of the Bounty Board affords for this proposed work in connection with that which it now performs, no less than the kind of property insured, justify the committee in expecting that these insurances might be effected at a less percentage, and also that there would result a profit-income applicable to increase the fund for the augmentation of livings, or to pay the expenses of the surveyors and registrars under 'The Ecclesiastical Dilapidations Act, 1871,' or for other Church purposes. The provision here recommended would be especially beneficial to the clergy by diminishing both the trouble and expense occasioned by the 55th section of the Act, for, as the governors would know the fact of the insurance and could secure the payment of the premium, a proviso might be added to the 55th section to the effect that the receipt for the premium of insurance be not exhibited at the visitation when the insurance has been effected at the office of the Bounty Board. The governors might also be empowered to accept the insurance against damage by fire of the whole fabric of the church on the applications of the churchwardens or others." I think that if such a mode of insurance is to be made compulsory, or, indeed, if it only be with a view to making it attractive, the terms of the insurance should not be higher than may be necessary to give proper security to the office ; there ought not to be any considerable profit. Again, it is suggested (3) "That the provisions of the Act in the case of complaints made by the patron, archdeacon, or rural dean be rendered applicable to those lay rectors, impropriators, or others, on whom rests the obligation of repairing the chancel or other portion of the church." For my own part I cannot see why such persons and property were not at the first included within the operations of the Act. We ought, I think, to petition that they may be. There is also (4) the serious question of the expense incurred in borrowing money from the Bounty Fund. If even a sum of only £100 is borrowed the cost of the mortgage for that amount is fixed by the Gilbert Acts at £10 15s., in addition to some payments to the officials of the diocese. This is, I am sure, a real grievance and an obstruction to the beneficial action of the governors. It seems, too, (5) that when a loan is required partly for repair (as under the new Act it may be) and partly for rebuilding, adding, or purchasing, it is believed there must be separate mortgage deeds for each amount borrowed. Surely one deed may be made sufficient. And (6) the machinery of negotiation with the Bounty Board is sadly cumbrous and expensive. Then (7) with regard to livings under sequestration. It is happily provided that the claim for dilapidations shall be a charge upon the net profits received by the sequestrator, second only to the claim for the stipends of the curates appointed to perform the duties. But there is this difficulty—that often a considerable time elapses before an amount sufficient to cover the estimated expense of the repairs is forthcoming from the benefice, and the work has to be done in part as the money from time to time comes in ; estimates made at the first cannot be depended upon after some time has elapsed ; great inconvenience is caused through the delay to the clergy-man in residence, the property suffers injury, and when there are tenants on the estate they suffer too, and the work itself being done piecemeal is done at greater cost. The amendment proposed is that the governors of the Bounty Office should be empowered to make a loan of the amount required to be repaid as the money comes in from the benefice by the sequestrator. In this way the works could be at once completed, and, as it seems, without placing any of the parties concerned at a disadvantage. Some amendment, too, (8) should be made in 45th section, where the surveyor is authorised himself to employ builders and contractors to execute the work which he will himself have to inspect. It is suggested that the treasurer of the Bounty Office, or that the sequestrator, should be the contracting party. It is a difficult point to determine, but certainly the surveyor should not be also the master builder. One principal intention of the Act, was (9) to give facilities to incumbents to put their houses in repair, and to receive certificates from the surveyor which should ensure them against ordinary dilapidation charges for five years. But the provisions to this end have been very little made use of in our diocese. And why is this ? Probably sometimes from indifference ; sometimes because the clergy have been unable to afford any considerable present outlay ; sometimes because those " who have their houses in fair condition and nicely furnished will not incur the trouble and turmoil of an inspection and subsequent repair." Very often too for another reason. Many a man desires to remove the burden of liability from his family, and yet he does not set in motion a machinery which he has no power subsequently to regulate, to check, or in any way to interfere with, and which may compel expenses of a magnitude such as when he entered on his benefice he had no reason to think he could have been made liable to. There are not a few who would be ready to put the buildings on their benefices in repair, and thus procure the five years' certificate, if they had permission to borrow the money for that purpose, and with the consent of the bishop and patron this may, by the Act, be done. But then arises the question whether it is just that an incumbent who has neglected the repairs for which he is liable should be allowed to burden the benefice by a mortgage, and so relieve his personal estate in the case of his own death or resignation. The rule in this particular is not the same in all dioceses. It has been suggested (10) that the surveyor's charges have deterred some men from availing themselves of this provision of the Act. It may be so; but I have no ground myself for believing this to have been the case. The work in our archdeaconry has been done well, and has on the whole given as much satisfaction as could be expected in the working out of what must often be considered an unpleasant business. It is essential to have a thoroughly competent surveyor, and such a person must be suitably as well as reasonably paid. If there should be any need to re-adjust the scale of payment or in any way to amend the terms of the engagement an opportunity will arise during the present autumn, when the period for which the present diocesan surveyors were appointed will have expired and the archdeacons and rural deans will be called upon to reconsider the present arrangements. With reference to an amendment of the Act every care should be taken to make its provisions for enabling incumbents to obtain a five years' certificate as simple as they can be made. A suggestion has been made (11) that it should be the duty of the surveyors when they make their first inspections to take a terrier or list of all the lands, buildings, &c., of a benefice—this terrier to be kept at the bishop's registry for use in future surveys, and a copy of it to be kept in the parish chest. Whether the surveyor should be the person to do this or whether it should be done by the minister, churchwardens, and other honest men of the parish as is ordered by the 87th Canon, such a terrier ought to be provided for every parish. Our surveyor tells me of a parish in this archdeaconry affording an instance of the necessity of looking after the property— the money value of the property of the benefice being not worth so much by £1,000 as it was 40 years ago, simply because the incumbents neglected during that period to hold a court. A suggestion has been made (12) by Mr. Crickmay, with a view to dealing with the difficult subject of fair wear and tear and progessive decay—that the surveyor should, with the other matters upon which he has to report under section 15 of the Act, report also "what sum of money shall be paid to the governors for and towards a contingent or rebuilding fund for such inherent decay, as it would not be expedient or possible to at once repair," and he also suggests (13) that some means of creating a Dilapidation Insurance Fund might be devised. He suggests also (14) that an addition should be made to the 58th section of the Act in regard to buildings standing on lands belonging to a benefice and comprised in any lease,

The last words of the section now stand : "It shall be lawful for the surveyor to inspect the buildings comprised in any such lease ;" he suggests that "a clause should be introduced requiring the surveyor to report on the state of such buildings, and the incumbents to serve notice to the lessees to perform the covenant of their lease ; the final certificate should not be given until these repairs had been executed by the lessee." He suggests also (15) an amendment in the 71st clause in order to allow the removal under proper authority not only of any building belonging to, or forming part of, any house of residence, but also of any buildings belonging to the benefice. And (16) one other suggestion of his I will mention, that in cases of vacant benefices treated under the Act, provision should be made for referring the question of fixtures to the diocesan surveyor, and in the event of his finding that they belong to the late incumbent, that he should value the same, and that the new incumbents should be empowered to borrow the amount of such valuation from Queen Anne's Bounty and purchase the fixtures, and thenceforth those fixtures, and all future fixtures, should belong to the benefice ; appeal from the diocesan surveyor's award to be provided as in the case of repairs. There are, however, many difficulties connected with such a proposal.

This subject of ecclesiastical dilapidation, and the position of the clergy with respect to recent legislation, has been very carefully treated of in a paper read before the Ruri-decanal Chapter of Wenlock, in the Diocese of Hereford, by the Rev. William Elliot, vicar of Cardington, and published by request. It is to be had at Messrs. Rivington's for sixpence. In this paper it is maintained that practically under the Act the responsibility of the clergy for dilapidation is now entirely unlimited and undefined, and, as being neither that of landlord or tenant, anomalous—that the court which has to assess for their damages consists of a single person, who, moreover, is not required to give any detailed account of the estimated expenditure, and that the surveyor is really the final arbiter. It is maintained that even before the surveyor there is no *locus standi* to plead mitigation of damages, and that from his award there is no satisfactory source of appeal, and scarcely any discretionary power in the hands of the Bishop. I think that at any rate in some of the particulars to which I have referred there are things which need consideration and amendment. Mr. Elliot is in favour of the course which we have adopted in this diocese—of having two surveyors rather than only one ; and of having men of the locality rather than men resident in London or at a distance. To show of what practical importance this matter is, let me state that Mr. Crickmay has been good enough to make me a return of the number of benefices which have been surveyed in this archdeaconry since the Act came into operation. There are some 250 benefices in this county, and of these in the years 1872 and 1873, and counting seven cases up to April in 1874, 60 surveys have been made. There have been vacant (by exchange 4, by resignation 14, by death 25) in all 43 ; under sequestration 6 ; with a view to a five years' certificate 11 ; this number together being very little short of the fourth part of the whole number of benefices in the archdeaconry. And five, in addition to these 60, were not visited either because there were no buildings or by direction of the Bishop. In 21 cases the repairs are completed. The amount of estimated expenditure upon the 60 benefices is about £11,000, and on the average about £183 on each, but, of course, there is the greatest variation in these amounts. A most useful little book upon this question is entitled "A Handy Book on the Ecclesiastical Dilapidations Act, 1871, with the Amendment Act, 1872," by Edward G. Bruton, F.R.I.B.A., Diocesan Surveyor, Oxon. Second Edition, with Analytical Index and printed forms. Rivington.

And now I would make some remarks in reference to

THE DIOCESAN SYNOD,

and to some things which have been considered by it. There have been four meetings of the Synod—one in the year 1871, and one in each successive year. We have had a full opportunity of considering its constitution and its procedure ; and the result is that very slight variations from its original form have been found desirable. The only change of any importance is referred to in the following resolution :—"That previous to the election of another Diocesan Synod, the Bishop be requested to direct that the relative number of lay representatives to be elected by the several parishes of the diocese be as follows :—For populations under 200, one ; 200 and under 1,000, two ; 1,000 and under 2,000, three ; 2,000 and upwards, four." As the lay members of the Synod are elected by the parochial representatives a more just proportion of influence in the election will thus be given to places containing a larger population. On this basis the election of the new Synod will take place in October. With reference to that election, I venture to express the hope that the clergy and church-wardens will not fail to see that representatives for their parishes are chosen. It is the Bishop's earnest desire to have the advice of the Church within his diocese fully and freely given—and it is only loyalty on our part to give a hearty acceptance to his invitation. It appears that on the last occasion some 45 parishes of the diocese made no return of lay representatives. In not a few cases this omission was made, though it was not a sufficient cause, because the parishes in question were very small; probably in some few instances out of objection to the Synod itself, and in some for no assignable reason. It should, however, be understood that every parish or district which appoints either one or two churchwardens is called upon by the Bishop to elect one or more lay representatives—to be members of the Ruri-decanal Synod and to take part in the election of the members of the Diocesan Synod. If such a case should occur—that both the clergy and churchwardens neglect, and upon application made to them decline to call a meeting for the election to take place, and if there should be laymen in that parish who desire to be represented, and have no means of securing that representation in a more orderly manner—the Bishop has expressed the hope that the laymen would meet and make an election as they best could. Among other words on this subject the Bishop said "There were some parishes which were under the immediate and entire influence of laymen, who had from the first disapproved of such a thing as this and had practically forbidden it, and that accounted for a certain number of parishes that had not sent representatives. There were also certain other parishes where the clergyman had taken a distinct tone of opposition and had thrown himself more or less into opposition to that which they had done, and where of course, as was not unnatural, lay representatives had not been elected. He should like to say, with respect to that, that of course they always sent to the clergyman and the churchwardens to direct that they should take measures for the election of lay representatives, but he did not imagine it depended on either clergyman or churchwardens to prevent any such election." And as a matter of justice to the lay members of the Church I think it is necessary to meet a few such extreme cases by this abnormal provision. One other matter touching the constitution of the Synod was discussed upon a motion being made "That to secure a more complete representation of the whole clergy of the diocese at future general elections of Synodsmen one of the clerical representatives elected by each rural deanry shall be elected from the non-beneficed clergy of the diocese." In regard

to this it was felt on the one hand that the freest access to
the Synod should be given to the clergy who are working
with us as curates, and on the other that the freest liberty
in selecting their representatives should be maintained
for the whole body of the clergy—and that by the
existing regulations this freedom was in both respects
secured. One other question of reform was raised, and
that related not to the constitution of the Synod but
to its procedure. It is a question, too, of considerable
importance. A motion was made "That on all occasions
of the votes on a division being called for the votes be
taken by orders"—that it should be the invariable rule
for the clergy and laity to vote in separate bodies. This,
in direct contradiction to the standing order of the
Synod, that ordinarily "all the members shall vote
together." This proposal so to change the procedure of
the Synod was declared to be lost by an immense
majority of the members present. And the Bishop said
that he looked upon it as a first principle that they
should blend together as one body unless a case of
necessity for otherwise acting arose. The present standing order provides "That before a division 15 clerical or
15 lay members may require that the vote be taken by
orders." I am inclined to think that liberty for the
exercise of this claim for a vote by orders should
be given after a division in cases where a motion has
been made and carried by a majority. The object of a
vote by orders in that case being to ascertain whether
the decision is acceptable to both clergy and laity—
whether practically through the consent of both orders
a resolution which has been passed could be put into
ure—for this could not profitably be done if either
order dissented from the conclusion. Other cases of
necessity for a vote by orders would now and then probably arise ; but, without here entering into the theory
of the matter, the practical result of the whole body, as
a rule, voting together has been so good that it would
surely be very unwise to change the standing order in that
respect.

THE REFORM OF CONVOCATION

came before us in the Synod, and the subject is
making at last considerable progress both in Convocation itself and the Church outside it.. As a sign
of the Archbishop's intention to move in the matter
a committee is again appointed to report upon the
election of proctors, and the subject is now quite certain
not to be dropped. In our own diocese the mode of
election being indirect and the number of representatives

small, is most unsatisfactory. If the plan proposed in Convocation is carried out the archdeaconries of the diocese will elect their own proctors—Sarum and Wilts one each and Dorset two ; and the electors will be the clergy in priests' orders, beneficed and licensed, in each archdeaconry. Happily our venerable Dean at the late election broke through the long standing custom of retaining the appointment of the Cathedral Proctor in the hands of the canons residentiary, and summoned the great Chapter to vote for a representative. No definite precedent for this mode of election could be found in the Cathedral records ; but the Dean was satisfied, from a consideration of the origin and history of the Cathedral, that such must have been the course of procedure in like matters in early days and that such for certain ought to be the course now. So many questions of grave importance are continually coming before Convocation that it becomes more and more of importance that it should be well constituted ; and I think that the clergy should not cease to petition for its reform.

PATRONAGE.

Another subject which came before us in Synod, and in which at last there seems to be a reasonable hope of reform, is that of Patronage. We have the weighty utterances of the Bishop of Lincoln upon it, and the subject has been entrusted for consideration to a committee of the House of Lords upon the motion of the Bishop of Peterborough, who, among other words in that great speech, was able to say that he made the motion with the unanimous concurrence of his right rev. brethren. We may surely hope that some of the most grave abuses in the matter will be removed. There is little desire among us to imitate the Church of Scotland and place all appointments to livings in the hands of the congregations. We are not in favour of popular elections. We certainly do not wish to see patronage separated from the tenure of property with which it is associated. Probably no system can be likely to work better than one like our own where patronage is widely distributed among several classes of patrons—and those patrons in very many cases having a special local interest—and it would be very difficult to say as a matter of fact that better men are chosen by one class of patrons than another. And it can be seen that the mind of the Church is now set in the right direction, and that, as a rule, great care is taken in the appointments. But there are sad exceptions, and the public advertisements still tell of much traffic in sacred things. Some things seem to stand in urgent need of revision—the sale of next presentations,—the sale of advowsons without limitation of the conditions of sale (e.g., in respect of the power to present immediately upon purchase and without restrictions to resell),—the anomalous position of donatives, which are made the medium of illicit transactions by reason of the exceptional circumstances under which they can be entered upon without presentation to the Bishop, and resigned without his having any power to stay the resignation—bonds of resignation and their force to deprive the Bishop of his power for reasonable cause to disallow resignation—the lack of safeguards against improper selection by patrons (as in the appointment of men too old, too young, or otherwise manifestly incompetent)—the discretion of the Bishop in respect of institution and the course of procedure by which the Bishop can exercise his right of objection to institute—the legal absurdities in the law of simony, and the facilities for its evasion and the form in which a presentee makes his declaration that he has not done anything which he knows to be simoniacal—the claim of parishioners to have some right of being heard in objection to an appointment—the mode under which exchanges are effected—these and no doubt other things in connection with our system of patronage need revision—and why may they not have that revision ? Their amendment would not touch the liberty of patrons in anything which rightly belongs to their trust—and it would not touch the great body of patrons who honestly exercise their trust, but it would check the course of that secret and illegitimate traffic which has so long with justice been our reproach. Happily, we have in our present Home Minister, Mr. Cross, a Churchman who takes the deepest personal interest in this matter, as we know by the fact that he himself, not long since, introduced into the House of Commons a Bill to abolish the sale of next presentations, and there are many other lay members of both Houses of Parliament equally anxious to promote the removal of abuses to which we have been referring. There was also a subject before us in Synod which had a close connection with our meeting to day.

ADMISSION OF CHURCHWARDENS TO OFFICE.

A Bill "to provide facilities for the admission of churchwardens to office" was introduced into Parliament by Mr. Monk. The point of it consisted in permission being given to churchwardens to make their declaration before their own clergyman or the rural dean instead of making it before the Ordinary at the visitation. There are other objections to such a course being adopted, but that which makes it most objectionable is that it would weaken the claim which now rests upon the officers of the parish church to attend the visitation. There is now once every year an occasion upon which an opportunity is given to persons in authority of trying to set right in a parish things which may be wrong. Grievances can be stated, and they are often removed upon this statement being made. The laity of the Church have their opportunity of appeal—the property of the Church is reported upon—presentments in respect of the performance of the duties of the clergy and of the character of the clergy are made—men in and under authority meet together for their common advantage. There may be much that might be better in the ordering of our visitations, and they are a fair subject for consideration, but I am persuaded that laymen would be very unwise if they were to allow themselves to be deprived of this opportunity of making themselves heard in the articles of enquiry which they are called upon to answer. When the Bill was introduced Mr. Cross was considerate enough to send circulars of enquiry to the Bishops, archdeacons, and others for their opinion upon the subject, and the replies he received were, I believe, very generally to the same effect as the resolution which was moved by Lord Nelson and carried, I think, unanimously in our Synod, and embodied in a petition to the House of Commons, which was presented by Mr. Cross, "That the Synod would be sorry to see the declaration now made by a churchwarden in the Court of the Bishop or Archdeacon made as this Bill would allow, without some very special reason, before the incumbent or Rural Dean." Lord Nelson said that he "regarded the attendance of churchwardens at the visitation courts as a matter of importance connected with the proper representation of the laity; and if they carelessly altered it merely for the purpose of meeting the convenience of a few churchwardens—although the system might be improved upon in another way, by making the work of the churchwardens more real—he believed they should go backwards and lose that hold which the Constitution at present gave the laity in the affairs of the Church." Several other subjects were before us in Synod; some of the most important I must altogether pass by, and on one or two others just say a word. A resolution was unanimously adopted that there ought to be annual collections in all parishes for the

DIOCESAN CHURCH SOCIETIES ;

and, surely, there ought to be such a collection everywhere, and I wish some special day were appointed for
the purpose. The subject of

PAROCHIAL FEES

had considerable discussion, and the report of the committee is in general circulation. It deals with things
material and external, but at the same time with things
which must be dealt with in daily life, and which ought
to have a settlement, upon which, as far as may be,
those who pay the fees and those who receive them may
be agreed. The table of fees which the committee are
instructed to draw up will be issued under the authority
of the Bishop, and I am persuaded that it will be found
in many places very useful. With regard to

LAY AGENCY

the principal points referred to were—First,

SUNDAY SCHOOL UNIONS

—which are found in some instances where they have been
at work in the diocese to have been helpful, and the Board of
Education is called upon to consider whether it can do anything to promote their increase and influence; and secondly,

LAY READERS.

In four parishes in this county, and one in Wiltshire,
appointments have been made. The license of the
Bishop is in the following terms :—

"George, by Divine permission Bishop of Salisbury. To our well
beloved in Christ,   Greeting.--We do by these presents grant
unto you, of whose faithfulness and competent knowledge we are
well assured, our commission to execute the office and perform
the duties of a Lay Reader, in the parish of   , in our
diocese and jurisdiction, on the nomination of the Reverend
          , and we do hereby authorise you to read the Word of
God, and explain the same to such persons in the said parish as
the incumbent shall direct; to read the appointed lessons in the
parish church, and also to read publicly in the schoolrooms, or in
any other place allowed by us, such portions of the morning and
evening service as we shall appoint and direct; and also to read
and expound some portion of Holy Scripture, or to read such
godly homily or discourse as the incumbent may approve. And
we exhort you to seek out persons not baptized, or sick, and to
make them known to the incumbent; and to give diligent heed
to prayer and the study of the Holy Scriptures, and to be an
example of godliness, sobriety, and brotherly love. And we do
hereby notify and declare that this our commission shall remain
valid, and have full force and authority, until either it shall be
revoked by us or our successors, or a fresh institution to the
benefice shall have been made and completed. And so we commend you to Almighty God, whose blessing and favour we humbly
pray may rest upon you and your work. Given under our hand
and seal, &c."

In one town parish this institution has been placed on a
fair and full trial by the appointment of four highly
qualified men. The rector of Bridport writes to tell

me that they have done, and are doing, and are likely to
do, good service for the Church; that they conduct
the service for the children in the schools, and feel that
they may at any time be called upon to read the lessons
in church, that he has heard of no single objection to
the institution from any person of the smallest consideration; that the men themselves seem to be deeply
impressed with the gravity of the commission, if he may
judge from the earnest way they are now working.
Other testimony to the same effect might be given.

ELEMENTARY EDUCATION.

I cannot altogether pass by the subject of elementary
education. The two points to which I would refer
are—1. The position of our schools under the Elementary Education Act; and 2. The diocesan inspection of
our schools in religious subjects. Persistent efforts are
made in Parliament to render obligatory the formation
of School Boards. No words, I think, can better give
the answer to these attempts than those in which Mr.
J. G. Talbot gave notice in the House of Commons that,
on the order for the second reading of the Elementary
Education (Compulsory Attendance) Bill, he would
move "That this House cannot entertain the question
of the universal establishment of School Boards until
perfect liberty of religious teaching shall be secured to
such Boards by the repeal of the 14th section of
the Elementary Education Act (1870), and until
such Boards are empowered to contribute to the support
of voluntary schools within their district, where it may
seem to be desirable." So long as it is by law forbidden
to the Church to use her Prayer Book in a rate-sup-
ported or rate-assisted school, so long must the Church
determine at whatever cost to maintain her own schools.
A few days since I was visited by a gentleman, Mr.
Allen, an agent of the Education league. He was on a
circuit of enquiry, and in a letter which reached me
just as he himself arrived, beginning "At the request of
Mr. Dixon, M.P. for Birmingham," he said that his object
was "to try and ascertain what were the real objections
of the clergy to the establishment of School Boards in
the country parishes." He said he wished to know "my
conclusions as to the attitude of the rural clergy towards
School Boards with compulsion." I think I left him
thoroughly persuaded that nothing could remove the
objection to the Boards short of the removal of the
bondage under which the Act now holds them by the
14th clause—a clause, be it always remembered, not in
Mr. Foster's original Bill, but, through the cleverness of
some and the weakness of others, let in as a compromise

afterwards—a clause not to be found in the Scotch Bill. From what he had himself seen too and heard, in the West he had found out the mistake of attributing this attitude to the rural clergy alone. He had learned that town clergy and town people were of the same mind, and that in these parts, as well as generally throughout the country, the doctrines of those who are at this time in a majority in Birmingham are not generally held. We have in this diocese abundant examples of town parishes and of country parishes in which great efforts on behalf of voluntary schools have been made, and these with the best results. But I think we have reason to point with especial satisfaction to the two chief towns of our diocese—Salisbury and Dorchester—as model districts, not single parishes, but far more difficult in this matter to deal with, sets of parishes, in which a zealous effort for the maintenance of definite religious teaching combined with full respect for liberty of conscience has resulted in the case of Dorchester (where to their great credit all personal and parochial considerations were for the purpose put aside) in a full supply for the town of all educational requirements without a Board, and in the other case of Salisbury, in the same full supply without the introduction of a single rate supported or rate assisted school. The last School Board election in Salisbury very clearly set forth the sentiments of men there. The four candidates who favoured the maintenance of the existing schools and definite religious teaching had, on the average, nearly 1,100 votes apiece in excess of the votes given to their four opponents, being a long way towards a proportion of three votes to one. Such contests as these have taken place throughout the country, and take place they must as long as the 14th Clause of the Act is law. Whether in London or in any place where there is a Board candidates will, as a rule, have to stand upon the view they take of the religious question. It must continue to be the duty of Churchmen, with others, to fight for the maintenance of full liberty of religious teaching—and this necessity arises in the main out of what I hold to be the unjust conditions imposed by that clause. Mr. Wilkinson, the secretary of the Board of Education, was visited by the same gentleman, and, in writing to me on the subject, he says "I told him, that as regards the clergy, the real obstacle was the Cowper Temple Clause, which was, in fact, a violation of religious liberty, forbidding the teaching of those catechisms and formularies which all concerned in the school desired to teach. If Mr. Dixon

desired to have the co-operation of the clergy in the
formation of School Boards let him go in for the repeal
of the clause in the name of religious liberty." As
regards landlords and tenants, apart from religious and
political reasons, there is naturally a disinclination to
overthrow an existing system, which works well and
gives at a small cost general satisfaction, in order
to introduce another—novel, expensive, and seriously
objected to by those who have hitherto done the
educational work of the country. Happily we can still
report that throughout the diocese of Salisbury men are
very generally of one mind in this matter. It is un-
necessary to refer to the 25th Clause of the Act, for it is
now clearly seen it can be defended on the plainest ground
even liberty for the poor man. With regard to School
Boards, it should be noticed that when statistics of the
number of the population under Boards are given there
is a risk of mistake as to the force of those statistics.
For instance, Lord Sandon the other night when moving
the vote for education says "Besides London, 104
boroughs representing a population of 5,500,000, out of
224 boroughs with a population of 6,531,892 were
under School Boards. There were also under School
Boards 717 civil parishes out of 14,072 with a population
of 12,913,387. The net result of this was that
10,494,507 of the population were under School Boards,
against 12,217,759 who were not in the same position,
and that by the middle of next year about half of the
population would be under Boards." Let it, however,
be clearly understood that although there may
perhaps by that time be Boards in places where
half the population reside, yet that by June, 1875
(when full school provision is expected to be making
or made), it is the outside calculation that in School
Board schools there will be provision for 500,000,
or one-eighth of the whole number thus provided
for. In the last returns to the end of 1873 the number is
but 125,000, and thus far short as yet of even this expected
provision for 500,000. But the truth is that School
Boards sometimes have no rate supported or rate
assisted schools; sometimes in large places they
have only one, or two, or very few schools belonging
to them. The School Boards may exist in those
places, but voluntary schools are often doing the
work of education. Witness Salisbury, Liverpool,
Manchester, Nottingham and numberless other
places, where these Board Schools are either none
or few. And this may remind us that in an Act
passed with the expressed intention of giving even op-

portunity for the establishment of voluntary and of School Board schools—there is this inequality. Liberty is given to a district to part with a voluntary system and introduce a Board. This may be done suddenly and unadvisedly, and be repented of; but, as our Bishop said in the Synod, *Vestigia nulla retrorsum.* A vast amount of good will be effected by the pressure which the Act has brought to bear upon the country for a due supply of schools; but there are one or two serious blots in the Act which must, as long as they continue to exist, prevent the general adoption of the Board School system. When discussing the subject with Mr. Allen I asked him whether he really could support what was called unsectarian teaching—whether such a thing could be defined, and, as a general system, worked out, and whether the League had not been compelled to reject such an idea. To which he replied that he was himself a Churchman, and entirely in favour of the Church teaching definitely her doctrines, only that he wished to dissociate that teaching from school work. But when reminded that this separation of religious instruction from school work was the very thing the people of this country would not consent to— that a secular school was scarcely known out of Birmingham—it appeared to me that he had to confess the weakness of the position of the League. I am not aware that I have met any Churchman who has upon religious grounds defended the principle of the 14th Clause; but in order to illustrate its natural results I must show you its working in a parish of Wiltshire—Donhead St. Mary. A School Board has just been introduced there consisting of five members. We cannot consider the question of the necessity for the introduction of this Board nor the question whether it may hereafter prove to be an institution acceptable to the parish when the consequences of its introduction are appreciated; but I will read you a paper publicly set forth by this new body. It runs thus:—

"A resolution of the Donhead St. Mary School Board, carried unanimously June 1st, 1874.

"That it is a matter of the highest importance that children educated at the public expense should be instructed in those principles of Christianity which are fundamental, yet not denominational; and that in the Donhead St. Mary School Board School the children shall, as far as their comprehension may permit, be instructed in such doctrines as are plainly set forth in the following passages from Scripture [I read the passages as they stand on the paper] :—

"'In the beginning was the Word, and the Word was with God, and the word was God.' 'And the Word was made flesh and dwelt among us.'—John i., 1, 14.

"'Christ was once offered to bear the sins of many.'—Heb. ix., 28. 'But Christ after He had offered one sacrifice for ever sat down on the right of God.'—Heb. x., 12.

"'All have sinned and come short of the glory of God.'—Rom. iii. 23. 'If any man sin, we have an advocate with the Father, Jesus Christ, the righteous: and He is the propitiation for our sins.'—I. John ii., 1, 2.

"'There is one God, and one Mediator between God and men, the Man Christ Jesus.'—I. Tim. ii., 5. 'The blood of Jesus Christ, God's Son, cleanseth from all sin.'—I. John i., 7. 'Neither is there salvation in any other, for there is none other Name under heaven given among men whereby we must be saved.'—Acts iv., 12.

"'Being justified by faith we have peace with God, through Jesus Christ.'—Rom. v., 1. 'Without holiness no man shall see the Lord.'—Heb. xii., 14.''

Here is a fair specimen of the religious programme of a School Board—of a thoroughly honest intention, no doubt, to set forth the best possible unsectarian creed, and children are to be instructed in such doctrines as are plainly set forth in these passages of Holy Scripture. Donhead St. Mary in the year of our Lord 1874, by five persons elected by ratepayers in a parish vestry promulges that which becomes a formulary to be the basis of religious instruction of the children of a parish of some 1,400 people. And the law places it in their hands to do this so long as no religious catechism or religious formulary which is distinctive of any particular denomination is introduced,—and the adjoining parish may issue another religious programme; and so on from parish to parish, if the system advances according to the varying religious mind and intelligence of the persons in the several vestries. And not to criticise the introductory statement beyond this—it must be observed that instruction is limited to the doctrines plainly set forth in certain given texts of Holy Scripture. The words themselves are words of truth in so far as they are truly and correctly taken from the Scriptures of God—but they are shorn of their strength because selected, isolated, and not interpreted. Even the passages themselves are in several instances only portions of sentences used apart from their context—in one or two instances, seriously mutilated and inaccurately quoted. But such a scheme, so unsound in its general principle, is not a subject for criticism in detail. And yet one must notice just this fact—that among other grave omissions not one of the selected texts sets forth the personality of God the Holy Ghost. Not even the doctrine of the Holy Trinity is set forth. Surely, brethren, we will spare no effort and no cost to escape from the introduction of such a loose system into our parishes; and let Churchmen who are not in difficulty themselves rise to the occasion and give help to those who are. The work is immediately pressing and important.

With regard to the other point—

THE DIOCESAN INSPECTION OF SCHOOLS

—you are aware that we have been of late in a state of transition from one system to another, and consequently there has been some confusion. I trust, however, that we are very near to the time when all will be simple. Already we have arrived at a satisfactory arrangement for the single examination and classification of the Pupil Teachers and Monitors of the diocese ; the results of that examination have been published with class and pass lists, and the Dorset National School Society last year gave gratuities to the successful candidates in our own county, and it has resolved to take that course this year. The society, I think, cannot do better than encourage the religious instruction of the future teachers of the country, and may fairly claim increased support to enable it to continue and increase its grants. But it is in respect of the Ordinary Scholars that we stand in need of a simplification of our system. One inspection and examination in the year is enough, and we have lately had two examitions—the one of the whole school, carried on by the Bishop's inspectors ; the other of selected scholars, under the Prize Scheme, the two examinations crossing each other and causing needless interruption of work and confusion. But it is intended at an early meeting of the Inspection Committee of the Diocesan Board (subject to the general approval of the Bishop) to propose an arrangement for consolidating the two plans into one, and this by a simple process. Mr. Wilkinson has shown me his proposal, and given me permission to make it known, that it may be considered and amended if thought desirable. I will extract from the Draft Regulations just enough to show the character of the proposal— " The diocesan inspection and examination of Church of England Elementary Schools in religious knowledge consists of two parts—the oral and the written ; both will be conducted by the Diocesan School Inspector at his annual visit to the school on the same day, and will follow, as far as possible, the syllabus for ordinary scholars, and for pupil teachers and monitors, aged 13 and upwards, respectively." The Diocesan School Inspector will arrange with the managers the precise day for the annual inspection, and will at that time conduct the oral examination. At the same time he will conduct the written examination. The ordinary scholars who are presented must be separated into three divisions according to age. The first to consist of those who are eight years of age and under ten ; the second of those who are ten and under twelve ; the third of those who are twelve and upwards, the age being reckoned from the 1st of March in each year. Papers of questions will be issued by the inspector to each of the examined in each division and year, the inspector giving different papers in different schools at his discretion. He will collect the papers at the close of the examination. He will examine the answers and award the marks at his convenience. The answers of the scholars that are classed and of all the pupil teachers and monitors will be forwarded by the diocesan inspector at the end of the year to the three examiners appointed by the Bishop—the Old Testament papers to one of the three, the New Testament to another, and the Prayer Book to the third. The three examiners will be appointed by the Bishop, for the purpose of preparing papers of the questions for the use of the diocesan inspectors, examining the answers of the scholars who have been classed by the inspectors, and those of the pupil teachers and monitors, and reporting on the same. Each of the three examiners will be at liberty to co-opt two colleagues, who will divide the work between them. There will be separate papers of questions on Old Testament, New Testament, and Prayer Book for each division and year of the examined, following the arrangement of the syllabus. These separate papers will be different in their contents, but equal in character. Thus a dozen different papers may be prepared for each subject (Old Testament, New Testament, and Prayer Book) in each division and each year, but they all will be as far as possible of equal difficulty. The examiners will mark the answers on a scale to be determined by themselves, and give the results on or before Lady Day in each year, thus : The names of the scholars, under their three divisions of age, will be arranged in two lists ; the first of those who are classed, and recommended for prizes of books, who will be placed in order of marks ; the second of those who are passed and recommended for certificates of merit, who will be placed in alphabetical order of schools. "The names of the pupil teachers and monitors of 13 under their several years of service, will be arranged in two lists ; the first of those who are classed and recommended for prizes of books, who will be placed in order of marks and receive a parchment

certificate of merit ; the second of those who are passed,
who will be placed in alphabetical order of schools."
We may, I trust, in some such way bring our diocesan
inspection plans into unity, and I see no reason why the
system should not in time be made as effectual as any
system of paid inspection would probably be.

BOARD OF MISSIONS.

And now, to pass in conclusion from the thought of
our home work and difficulties, let me ask you heartily
to support the Bishop of the diocese in the endeavour he
is making to institute a great diocesan festival on behalf
of the Foreign Missions of the Church of England. In
the circular letter we have received from him, among
other things the Bishop says—"It has been my most
anxious desire ever since I have been in the diocese to lift
the subject of Christian Missions above the comparatively
narrow sphere of societies, excellent and necessary as they
are, and to unite together, in what I consider a still
loftier way, all who recognise the duty of Church people
of every school within the Church of England, to
further the spread of the Gospel among mankind." And
again—"This proposed festival is, so far as I am aware,
the first great diocesan effort of the kind made in England. It is not to be regarded as a joint meeting of the
two societies, but as a meeting of Church people, held
independently of societies, for the encouragement of the
missionary spirit in the Church." I do myself most
heartily concur in the desire and sentiments which are
here expressed, and I am persuaded that the proposal is
sound and good in itself, and moreover that it is in
harmony with the desires and yearnings of the vast body
of our thoughtful and faithful laity as well as clergy.
The Board of Missions has authority to state that the
Bishop's invitation is intended for every person, lay as
well as clerical, in his diocese. And the clergy are
asked to give the widest possible circulation to it. Most
unfeignedly do I desire to see the independent efforts of
our great missionary societies maintained and extended,
and with the deepest thankfulness to Almighty God we
must all acknowledge the real increase during the past
year which both our great societies are able to record—
an increase in the number of those whom God has sent
as labourers, and an increase in the means of support-
ing them. In the mission field itself the way for
Christian enterprise is being made in almost every
direction, by God's Providence, more open and unre-
stricted, and the call to enter upon it more encouraging.
Can we do better than answer this gift of God by

renewed zeal in the same great cause, and by that which
is in God's sight most blessed, and in the furtherance of
the work itself most effectual—by an effort in unity such
as the spirit of charity can alone produce. In the year
1372 a call was made by our chief pastors to united
intercession on an appointed day on behalf of the Foreign
Missions of the Church ; and the Churches in full communion with us throughout the world, as far as they
were able to do so, observed that day, and many other
men, unhappily more or less outwardly separated from
us, joined in that common prayer. Everywhere there
was an agreement as to what men should ask, and the
thing they agreed to ask for was according to promise
granted. In the year following (last year) we
again met together on the same behalf, and then it
was that the Archbishop of Canterbury, upon consideration of what God had manifestly given in answer to the
prayer of His Church, recommended that another day
should be observed as one of thanksgiving as well as
prayer. Surely among some things which cause anxiety
and bespeak self-will and pride those days of agreement
in intercession and thanksgiving speak hopefully. They
tell of Faith and Charity in the Church. And let us
claim to have such a time continued to us—whether
eventually it may be determined to assign any one of
the Church's Rogation days as most suitable for this great
purpose, or whether it may be thought better to take
any other fixed time of the Church or to select from
year to year a special day. Only let a zealous and
charitable missionary spirit be alive in the hearts of
Churchmen, and many of the practical difficulties and
hindrances which arise out of the imperfections and in-
firmities and petty jealousies of men, and which too often
mar the great common work, will be overcome. There
is ample room in the world for an exercise of the
diversities of the gifts and operations of individuals,
and of societies, too. There is at the same time a necessity
that the Church should do all things decently and in
order. It is from this consideration that I am glad to
believe that, as for some lesser purposes in this diocese
we have a Diocesan Board, so more extensively for the
Church of England generally we are to have a Church
Board of Foreign Missions. The constitution of this
Board has been under the consideration of a committee
of Convocation, and it is being constituted in such a
way that the several dioceses of England and Wales
may be represented upon it by their Bishops and by
some clerical and lay representatives ; and in our own
diocese the Bishop has, I am told, already appointed

Earl Nelson and the Rev. Prebendary Baker to represent
us. It is also intended to seek co-operation with our
brethren in Ireland and Scotland, and with the Colonial
and other Churches within our communion. It is felt
there should be some such central and influential body,
in which, on a level higher than that of societies,
members of those societies may from time to time
meet on common ground and survey and take
counsel upon the needs and opportunities of the mission
field—where also those many important missions which
are not in any special relation with the two great
missionary societies may be brought into consideration
with a view to the general and combined advance of the
kingdom of God in the world. This subject of Foreign
Missions leads me to recommend to your notice a
valuable and interesting, though very small, publication
of the Society for the Propagation of the Gospel in
Foreign Parts, entitled "Present Results and Future
Prospects of Existing Missions in India"—extracted
from a statement of the progress of India, prepared
at the India Office, and based on the administra-
tive reports and other information received from
India, and printed by order of the House of Commons, April 28th, 1873. Things are here told of
India which, though yet indeed but too little, are
such as faith alone in days gone by could see and
pray for. There is evidently a shaking of the nations in
that strange land and the rulers of the earth bear witness
to it. I will only mention two points out of many to
which this statement refers. One is this ; speaking of
the Church of England and other Protestant missionaries,
it says : " This large body of European and American
missionaries, settled in India, bring their various moral
influences to bear upon the country with the greater
force, because they act together with a compactness
which is but little understood. Though belonging to
various denominations of Christians, yet, from the
nature of their work, their isolated position, and their
long experience, they have been led to think rather of
the numerous questions on which they agree than of
those on which they differ, and, they co-operate heartily
together. Localities are divided among them by
friendly arrangements, and, with few exceptions, it is a
fixed rule among them that they will not interfere with
each others' converts and each others' spheres of duty.
School-books, translations of the Scriptures and religious
works, prepared by various missions, are used in common ;
and helps and improvements secured by one mission are
freely placed at the command of all"—and more to the

same effect. And this charitable forbearance and united
effort are greatly blessed, as these other words shew :—
"Taking them together, these rural and aboriginal populations in India, which have received a large share of the
attention of the missionary societies, now contain among
them a quarter of a million native Christian converts.
The principles they profess, the standard of morals at
which they aim, the education and training which they
receive, make them no unimportant element in the
empire which the Government of India has under its
control. These populations must greatly influence the
communities of which they form a part ; they are
thoroughly loyal to the British Crown ; and the experience
through which many have passed has proved that they
are governed by solid principle in the conduct they
pursue. But the missionaries in India hold the opinion
that the winning of these converts, whether in the cities
or in the open country, is but a small portion of the
beneficial results which have sprung from their labours.
No statistics can give a fair view of all that they have
done. They consider that their distinctive teaching, now
applied to the country for many years, has powerfully
affected the entire population. This view of the general
influence of their teaching, and of the greatness of the
revolution which it is silently producing, is not taken
by missionaries only. It has been accepted by many
distinguished residents in India, and experienced
officers of the Government ; and has been emphati-
cally endorsed by the high authority of Sir Bartle
Frere. Without pronouncing an opinion upon the
matter, the Government of India cannot but acknowledge the great obligation under which it is laid
by the benevolent exertions made by these 600 missionaries, whose blameless example and self-denying
labours are infusing new vigour into the stereotyped life
of the great populations placed under English rule, and
are preparing them to be in every way better men and
better citizens of the great empire in which they dwell."
There is indeed much cause to thank God that such
words as these have been written. But an appeal has just
reached us from that same great land of India which
solemnly warns us against the mistake of over-estimating
the amount of past success. The three Indian Bishops
of Calcutta, Madras, and Bombay have written a letter
to the Archbishops, Bishops, and clergy of Canterbury
and York in Convocation assembled, in which they
plead most earnestly for immediate and great help.
They tell us that the season is critical, that they are
convinced the future of India depends very much on

what is done for it by the Church of England during
the next few years ; that India in the present century
is passing through a state of disintegration—that the
people are being carried, almost without a will, and,
as if by a tide of circumstances, from a past, to
which their hearts cling with regret, to a future which
is still unknown and undiscernible. They say that
many thousands have become believers in Christ, and
give proofs of stability and independence ; that converts
are added in an increasing proportion, and the number
of native clergy steadily augmenting. But they add—
"In India we are dealing with millions, not with thousands, and we should mislead you if we gave you to
understand that any deep general impression has been
produced, or that the conversion of India is imminent."
And then, after other words, they say : "We state this,
not at all to disparage such work as has been done, and
still less to discourage efforts, but because we feel bound
to describe to you India as it is, and to dispel any
illusions of marked religious success which might arise
out of the statements and reports of official and other
eminent authorities, though these in reality describe
social or political results rather than religious victories.
The opportunity is really great, and our hope is strong
that you will send us men of large hearts and gifted
minds, who have the wisdom and the power to take
advantage of it. Where such men have been at work
the results have been encouraging. Apostolic men,
doing Apostolic work, have left an Apostolic mark
wherever they have laboured. Only Faith is needed, and
the will to put forth those inexhaustible resources
which are stored within our Church. Then this work,
as great as ever any portion of the Church was called on
to perform, may be accomplished, and 240,000,000 of the
human family, subject to our tolerant and just Government,
will be raised out of a vile degradation into the glorious
Communion of Saints. We appeal, then, to you,
brethren beloved in Christ, and we cry to you in God's
Name to help us." These Bishops of India claim our
intercession, our men, men of our finest gold, our
devoted women, our money, and they conclude their
touching appeal with these words—with which I will
myself conclude :—"We need not say more. We speak
to you as with the mouth of hundreds of millions. We
bring the wants of these innumerable souls before you,
and lay them down beneath your eyes, before your feet.
Give, we pray you, to the consideration of their claims
upon the Church of England that wisdom which so
richly fills you, that sense of duty which is the brightest

characteristic of the English people ; above all, that faith in your Lord's support which can remove mountains ; that highest grace of Love without which all other gifts are but vain. On the colonial world—in America, in Africa, in Australia, in the Islands of the Pacific—you have bestowed, during the life of one generation, the Church of God, in the fulness of its order and the completeness of its gifts ; building it on the foundation of the Apostles, and of Christ its corner-stone. A work vaster, and far more difficult is now before you ; and it is not we, but God Himself, and Jesus Christ, His Son, who calls you to it. It may be the work of the age— the work which, when the history of this and of the twentieth century is written, will shine conspicuous above all which art and science (in this great era) have accomplished. Consider it with the breadth of mind and largeness of heart which it demands from you." And I would say with them to you, my brethren—May the Father, the Son, and the Holy Spirit be with you to guide your counsels and to shape your ends—Amen.

The Bishop of Lincoln on the Public Worship Regulation Bill.

A PLEA FOR TOLERATION BY LAW IN CERTAIN RITUAL MATTERS WITH REFERENCE TO "THE PUBLIC WORSHIP REGULATION BILL."

A conversation arose on Wednesday last in the Upper House of the Convocation of Canterbury, on the presentation of a petition from some distinguished laymen, praying that sufficient time might be given to the clergy for the consideration of the Public Worship Regulation Bill now before Parliament, and I now wish to state somewhat more fully what was briefly expressed by me on that occasion.

It is agreed on all sides that the constitution and modes of procedure of our Ecclesiastical Courts require amendment. It is also a general opinion that a remedy is urgently needed for evils and abuses prevailing in some of our churches, in the ritual of Divine service, whether by excess or defect.

The Public Worship Regulation Bill is based on these two acknowledged facts.

We need not now enquire whether measures are not equally required for the correction of ecclesiastics, whether bishops or clergy, who may offend by unsoundness of doctrine or viciousness of life ; and whether such offences might not be dealt with in the same legislative enactment as that which concerns the public worship of the Church.

The question now submitted for consideration is—

Whether the Public Worship Regulation Bill does not require the complement of certain co-ordinate provisions, in order to render it a safe and salutary enactment at the present time.

The Bill is of a stringent, coercive, and penal character. Under its operation a bishop might find himself to be divested of his character and influence as a spiritual father, and be constrained as a judge, sitting with assessors in his consistory court, to enforce on the clergy of his diocese a rigid uniformity under severe penalties, in certain ritual matters which have hitherto been regarded by many as doubtful, but which may hereafter be decided in one exclusive sense by Ecclesiastical Courts.

There seem to be two important principles to be kept steadily in view at the present juncture.

On the one side, it is the duty of a Church not to surrender its power of toleration in things of question able obligation, especially in a free age and country like ours, and at a time when private judgment, and even individual waywardness, have been allowed to manifest themselves in varieties and extravagances unknown for two centuries. Remedies good in themselves may become relatively bad by reason of the state of the patient to whom they are applied.

We need the higher and nobler functions of charity and equity to temper the rigour of law, and to prevent law from degenerating into injustice.

On the other hand, while a large measure of liberty is conceded, care is to be taken that it may not be abused by individuals into an occasion of unbridled licentious-ness.

The result of these two propositions is that the measure of liberty ought to be determined by law.

In other words, it ought not to be left to individual clergymen to choose by an eclectic process what rites and ceremonies they please from ancient, mediæval, or modern Churches, and to import them into their own churches, and to impose them on their own congrega-tions, which would lead to endless confusion ; but the Church of England, exercising that authority which belongs to all national Churches, ought to define and declare publicly by her synodical judgments what things in her services are to be regarded as obligatory and what may be considered as indifferent. And she ought, as an Established Church, to seek for legal sanction from the Crown and from Parliament, for these her authoritative definitions and declarations.

These were the principles on which our Book of Common Prayer was framed and revised.

To illustrate this by examples—

The eastward position of the celebrant at the prayer of Consecration in the Holy Communion has been con-demned and prohibited by the Court of Final Appeal. And the position at the north end has been declared to be the legal one.

If this question were to be argued again this judg-ment would probably be re-affirmed.

My reasons for this opinion are as follows :—

The Church of England in her rubric at the beginning of her office for the Holy Communion recognises two positions of the communion table as equally lawful. The table may stand "in the body of the church." This is the first position which it specifies. And in this case it would stand long-wise, *i.c.*, parallel to the north and south walls of the church.

This was the position of the table in most parish churches during the seventeenth century, and at the last review; as appears from the 7th canon of the Convocation of 1640—Archbishop Laud's Convocation.

In this case it is certain that the celebrant did not occupy an eastward position, but stood on the north side of the table with his face to the south.

The second lawful position of the holy table was "in the chancel" at the east end ; and there it stood cross-wise, *i c.*, from north to south.

This was its position "in most cathedral churches, and in some parochial churches," as the same canon declares ; and has now become general.

That in cathedrals the celebrant stood at the north end (called the north side in the rubric, which is purposely framed so as to suit both positions of the table) is clear from the testimony of the continued and uniform usage of all cathedral churches to the present times. In the case of a very few cathedrals the eastward position has been introduced within the last ten years. But I am speaking of the practice up to the beginning of the present century.

The engraving which Laud's bitter enemy, William Prynne (who would gladly have convicted him of any practice regarded by Puritans as Papistical), published of the arrangement of the archbishop's private chapel (London, 1644, p. 123), where the cushion for the celebrant (for a cushion there was) is placed at the north end of the table, leads to the same conclusion.

This is further demonstrated by the well-known rubric of the non-jurors (no favourers of Protestantism) in their Prayer Book, where the words "before the table" are explained to mean "the north side thereof."

Being desirous of showing dutiful obedience to the laws of the Church of England, I have earnestly endeavoured to persuade the clergy of the diocese of Lincoln to consecrate the Holy Communion at the north side of the table, so as to be able more readily, in compliance with the rubric, "to break the bread before the people.'

But does it follow that a Bishop should desire to be armed with powers (such as are given him by the present Bill) to enforce this law ? And does it also follow that he should wish to be compelled, on the complaint of a parishioner (as contemplated in the Bill), to enforce it ?

Nothing less, for by such a course he would probably drive from their cures some of the most zealous clergymen in his diocese, and produce a schism in the Church.

He would indeed be thankful for uniformity, if he could have it as well as unity; but if he cannot have both he would not sacrifice unity to uniformity; this would be to prefer the letter to the spirit.

But would he wish to leave things as they are?

No; for at present (to specify the same example) a clergyman who consecrates in the northern position is prone to condemn a brother who holds to the eastern position as doing what is illegal; and thus strifes are engendered destroying the peace and efficiency of the Church.

Where, then, is the solution?

Let either position of the celebrant be declared by authority to be lawful; in other words, let the position be pronounced by law to be indifferent. The position of the holy table itself is already declared by law to be indifferent. It may be in the chancel, and it may be in the body of the church.

Why not also the position of the celebrant at the holy table?

As a matter of fact, this solution has already been applied in the sister Church of America. That Church glories in the name of Protestant. It styles itself "The Protestant Episcopal Church." But it recognises the eastward and northern position as equally lawful; indeed, in some dioceses, another position, which is commended by its high antiquity—namely, on the east side of the holy table, with the face of the celebrant looking westward—is also permitted.

Why should not we do the same in the Church of England?

Each of those two former positions of the celebrant has its own special significance. The one represents the Divine grace and gift to man. The other expresses man's plea for mercy and acceptance with God. The one looks manward from God; the other looks Godward from man. The one position exhibits the benefits of communion with Christ; the other commemorates—and pleads the merits of—his one sacrifice for sin. It might be well that the Church, by permitting and authorising both those positions, should set before her people this double aspect and meaning of that blessed sacrament, and thus, even by relaxing the strictness of ritual uniformity, preserve and represent unity and completeness of doctrine concerning those holy mysteries.

The third position of the celebrant, which is perhaps the most ancient of all (that at the east side of the holy table with his face looking westward to the people), might also safely and rightly be permitted.

We should derive benefit from this variety. We should have a fuller view of the manifold significance of the Holy Eucharist from these three positions, just as we have a clearer view of the Gospel from having four Gospels than if we had only one Gospel.

The Church of Rome authorises two positions, the one looking eastward, the other westward, so that the eastward position ought not to be condemned as distinctively Roman. It is also sanctioned by Lutheran Churches.

I have said that, in my opinion, the Purchas judgment, condemning the eastward position of the celebrant, would probably be reaffirmed.

I am not so sure that this would be the case with that part of the judgment which, while it prescribes the use of the cope by the celebrant in cathedrals on great festivals, condemns the use of a distinctive Eucharistic dress by the celebrant in parish churches. I am rather disposed to think that the use of such a vestment might hereafter be pronounced to be obligatory.

If this should happen to be the case—and to say the least it is probable—what would be the predicament of a Bishop if "The Public Worship Regulation Bill," now before Parliament, became law?

He would be obliged to enforce the northern position on the celebrant, and also to require him to wear a distinctive Eucharistic vestment.

Would this be acceptable to either of the two great parties in the Church?

Might it not produce a double rupture in his diocese?

Where, therefore, again let us ask, is the solution?

Let us no longer waste our energies on vexatious and ruinous litigation (we have lately been told in Parliament that two lawsuits cost as much as would have built and endowed a parish church); but let the National Church of England declare by authority that a simple distinctive dress for the celebrant at the Holy Eucharist is permissible, but not to be enforced upon any. This also has already been done in some dioceses of America.

It has, indeed, been objected that the solution is more easy in America than in England, because the constitution of the American Church is congregational rather than parochial, and that nothing can there be introduced into the services of the Church on the mere motion of an individual minister against the wish of the congregation.

But it may be replied that in our great towns the congregational system, as distinct from the parochial, prevails as much as in America; and that in rural districts in America the system is parochial.

In that country there is a double safeguard against extravagances; first, the consent, duly ascertained and expressed, of the communicants of congregation or parish; and next, the sanction of the ordinary. Both these guarantees against innovations and excesses may be obtained in the Church of England, as well as in that of America.

A few years ago the adoption of the surplice in the pulpit in some parish churches produced a commotion. And why? Because it was an innovation introduced by individual clergymen, and because the people were naturally uneasy and suspicious, from the apprehension that other innovations might follow in rapid succession without limitation. But now that the surplice has been declared by authority to be a lawful vestment the objections have passed away.

Also, as soon as the cope was pronounced by the Final Court of Appeal to be the lawful vestment of the celebrant at certain times and places no exception was taken to its use. But, I suppose, we should not wish it to be enforced in all our cathedrals under penalties by law, as it may be if the present Bill should pass.

Again, at the present time a bishop may at his discretion require two full services on a Sunday in any church in his diocese; and he is generally presumed to have a discretionary power of enforcing daily service and the observance of saints' days and holy days, and the administration of the sacrament of baptism after the second lesson, and public catechising.

But if the present Bill were to become law it would seem that any incumbent "who failed to observe the directions in the Book of Common Prayer relating" to these and other things (I quote the words of the Bill) might be subject to severe penalties, and even to suspension.

I have no wish that such things as these should be declared indifferent; but I refer to them as showing that there is, and must be, some discretionary power lodged somewhere; and it will be difficult to say where it can be vested if not in the ordinary.

But there are one or two other ritual matters (and I do not think that there need be more) which might, I conceive, be declared by law to be indifferent, and if this course were pursued then the danger of a schism, which might be incurred if the present Bill passes without any moderating and qualifying provisions, would be averted, and the Bill itself might be made acceptable to the great body of the faithful and loyal clergy and laity of the Church of England.

In adopting such a course we should be treading in the steps of our own reformers, and of those who revised the Prayer-book at the Restoration.

The doctrine contained in the Prayer-book is unalterable, because it is the faith revealed in Holy Scripture, and received by the Primitive Church.

But the Reformers altered the Ritual of the Church no less than three times in the course of twenty years ; and in the preface which is prefixed to that book at the last review, about 200 years ago, and which is due to one of the most judicious of English prelates, Bishop Sanderson, it is affirmed that " it hath been the wisdom of the Church of England, ever since the first compiling of her public liturgy, to keep the mean between the two extremes, of too much stiffness in refusing, and of too much laxness in admitting, any variation from it ;" and it " is but reasonable that, upon weighty and important considerations, according to the various exigencies of times and occasions, such changes and alterations should be made therein as to those that are in place of authority should from time to time seem either necessary or expedient.

It may, therefore, be presumed that our Reformers and our revisers of the Book of Common Prayer would, as wise, learned, and pious men, carefully contemplating the altered circumstances of the times and the condition of the Church in these days, be the first to relax some of the stringent laws of our ritual, and to pronounce certain things to be indifferent by law, in order that they might promote those high and holy purposes of faith, worship, and morals for which the Prayer-book was framed, and which are paramount to all rites and ceremonies of human institution.

Let me here submit another suggestion. At former epochs in our Church history, when alterations in our Liturgy were contemplated, leading persons on different sides were summoned to a friendly conference. Such was the Hampton Court Conference, at the beginning of the reign of James the First, and the Savoy Conference at the Restoration. Much benefit was thus derived from a free interchange of opinion. A conference at the present time of those eminent men in our Church of opposite parties, who have been too much estranged from one another, would probably lead to mutual concessions ; and a result might be obtained which, without enforcing obnoxious practices on either, as things necessary to be observed, might lead to a liberal toleration, limited by law, of things permitted to be done under certain conditions, and thus liberty might be secured without degenerating into licentiousness.

The report of the Lower House of Convocation of June 5, 1866, and the reports of the Royal Commission on Ritual, might supply means and materials for this peaceful adjustment.

If such a course as has now been traced out were followed there is reason to believe that, under God's good Providence, our strifes would be appeased, and law and order be restored, and the Church would be free to devote her energies to the performance of her divinely appointed work—that of waging war against ignorance and sin, and of diffusing the Gospel of Christ at home and abroad, and of promoting God's glory and the temporal and eternal welfare of mankind.

C. LINCOLN.

H. SPICER, COUNTY PRINTER, DORCHESTER.

www.ingramcontent.com/pod-product-compliance
Lightning Source LLC
Chambersburg PA
CBHW021428090426
42739CB00009B/1402